CHOOSE YOUR OWN CAREER ADVENTURE

BROADWAY

Monique Vescia

Created and produced by
Bright Futures Press, Cary, North Carolina
www.brightfuturespress.com

Published by
Cherry Lake Publishing, Ann Arbor, Michigan
www.cherrylakepublishing.com

Photo Credits: cover, Shutterstock/Tracy Whiteside; page 5, Shutterstock/Diego Cervo; page 5, Shutterstock/ Phase 4 Studios; page 5, Shutterstock/Steve Wood; page 7, Shutterstock/d13; page 8, Shutterstock/jiunn; page 9, Shutterstock/Stokkete; page 9, Shutterstock/atanasijal; page 13, Shutterstock/Photographer.eu; page 13, Shutterstock/Valentyn Volkov; page 15, Shutterstock/Sergey Nivens; page 17, Shutterstock/Tito Wong; page 17, Shutterstock/Rajesh Narayanan; page 19, Shutterstock/aerogondo2; page 21, Shutterstock/Gleb Stock; page 21, Shutterstock/Andrey Burmakin; page 23, Shutterstock/Gleb Stock; page 25, Shutterstock/ bikeriderlondon; page 25, Shutterstock/Mny-Jhee; page 27, Shutterstock/bikeriderlondon; page 29, Shutterstock/Ververidis Vasilis; page 29, Shutterstock/Lance Bellers.

Library of Congress Cataloging-in-Publication Date

CIP has been filed and is available at catalog.loc.gov.

Printed in the United States of America.

BROADWAY

Welcome to the bright lights of Broadway!

Audiences flock to 40 professional theaters, each with at least 500 seats, in the vicinity of Broadway and 42nd Street in New York City. Why do they go? To see incredible live productions, such as *The Lion King*, *Wicked*, and *Phantom of the Opera*. These plays feature huge casts, with complicated dance routines and catchy show tunes. The sets are dazzling and inventive, and the talent is top-notch.

Many Broadway theater buildings have splendid interiors, adorned with mammoth chandeliers and gold-leaf decorations. No wonder 12 million tickets are sold every year!

For anyone working in the world of theater, Broadway represents the cream of the crop, the top of the heap. It is a big deal to see your name in lights on Broadway! With so many in the performing arts eager to make it to the Broadway stage, or backstage, you can see why Broadway would be a cool place to work.

Here's your chance to see your name in lights on the **Great White Way**. Pick you favorite career, and let your Broadway adventures begin!

TABLE OF CONTENTS

DIRECTOR

Seeking seasoned theater director for new Broadway production. Candidate must bring unique vision to the script. Responsibilities include casting actors, and collaborating with set and costume designers. Communication skills are key! Cool, calm, and collected leader preferred. Must work closely with the stage manager to bring the story to life.

- *Ready to take on this challenge?*
  Turn to page 6.

- *Want to explore a career as a Musical Director instead?*
  Go to page 9.

- *Rather consider other choices?*
  Return to page 4.

Explore the world of musical theater at **http://bit.ly/ HighSchoolMusicalGuide**.

From Script to Broadway Hit

As **director** of a Broadway play, your work begins months before the **premiere** as you read through the **script** nearly a million times (OK, maybe not quite that many—but a lot!). Each time you read it, you make notes of creative ideas for how to stage it.

This preparation is a big help to you when actors come in to **audition**. You know exactly what you're looking for and assemble the perfect cast. You also spend a lot of time sharing ideas with a producer and the stage manager. Success depends on all the cast and crew sharing the same vision for the play.

Once any kinks are worked out, the set and costume designers get busy creating the spectacular onstage world, where your play will take place. Lighting designers and other theater technicians also add their creative spark to the production. Everything they do must meet with your approval since you're the play's director!

Now, finally, it is time for **rehearsals** to begin!

How Stars Are Born

As you follow the rehearsal from your spot in the third row, you notice the male lead is having trouble with an important **monologue**. You ask him to try it again, but this time you have him move diagonally across the stage when he's midway through his speech. That small shift in **blocking** makes a big difference. You also direct him to say one line with more excitement. The stage manager keeps track of these changes, adding them to the script.

After each rehearsal, you give the cast members feedback on their progress and motivate them to give their best performance. You respect that people, including actors, sometimes have fragile egos, so you've learned to be diplomatic. Even if it's true, you don't tell an actor, "Your big love scene in Act Three was as romantic as a grocery list!" Instead you say, "Good start. Next time, let's crank up the heat in the third act."

Opening Night Jitters

Everyone in the cast and crew works long hours to tighten the production. On some days, everything seems to go wrong and you might wonder if the whole production is cursed! Nerves fray, but you keep everyone focused and feeling positive about the play.

Before you know it, opening night arrives. And you tell the cast right before the curtain rises, "**Break a leg**!"

Your Director Career Adventure Starts Here

EXPLORE IT!

Use your Internet search skills to find out more about the following:

Famous Broadway directors   The Tony Awards

Classic Broadway plays   History of Broadway

Famous Broadway actors

TRY IT!

Give an Old Plot New Life

The award-winning Broadway musical *West Side Story* re-imagined Shakespeare's tragic play *Romeo and Juliet*, spinning the tale into a rivalry between two teenage street gangs on New York's Upper West Side during the 1950s. What if you were asked to update a favorite classic book or movie? How would you give it a modern twist?

Take Notes

Attend a local theater production at a nearby school or community theater (check local newspapers for upcoming events). If that's not possible, watch a movie on TV or online. During the show, jot down comments about the production—the parts you liked best and any ideas for improvement.

MUSICAL DIRECTOR

Can you play piano, read music, find the beat? Broadway musical production seeks talented musical director. Duties include auditioning talent, coaching singers, and directing rehearsals with musicians. Conducting the pit orchestra with pizazz during performances a must. Perfect pitch is a plus!

- *Ready to take on this challenge?*
  Turn to page 10.

- *Want to explore a career as a Producer instead?*
  Go to page 13.

- *Rather consider other choices?*
  Return to page 4.

Have fun learning the basics of conducting an orchestra at **www.sfskids. org/conduct.**

High and Low Notes

Talented singers are lined up inside (and often even winding around the outside) the theater to audition for the starring roles in your new musical production. You are the **musical director** and you're looking for singers with real range, those who can hit both the high and low notes. Of course, musical talent isn't enough. The stars of this show must be able to act and dance too! In the entertainment business, they call talent like this the "triple threat." When you find performers who are talented in all three areas, the only thing left to say is, "When can you start?"

Assembling the Orchestra

You also have to hire 20 musicians to fill the **pit orchestra**. You need musicians who can play woodwind and brass instruments, plus someone on piano and keyboards. Some theaters have larger orchestra pits, but yours happens to have room enough for only 20 musicians. And since your current musical score calls for more than 20 different instruments, you look for musicians who can double up and play more than one. The result is an amazing array of talent making beautiful music together.

Now about that score, which was created by a famous **composer**, who wrote the music, and a **lyricist**, who wrote the words. It's spectacular! Even so, matching the music to the action on stage takes a little focused attention on your part. You need to rework certain sections of the score to keep the production on track. This is probably one of your favorite parts of the job!

Raise the Baton

After weeks of preparation, it is finally opening night! Before the show, you check in with the singers. Does anyone have a cold or a raspy voice from a previous performance? Then it's down to the orchestra pit to make sure all the musicians are in place and warming up.

Dressed in your tuxedo and holding your conductor's baton, you wait for the theater director's signal to start. A little red light next to your podium in the orchestra pit blinks on when it's time to begin. The musicians all watch you attentively, and the audience settles into an excited silence. Above your head, the whole stage spreads out in front of you. You love your job—you have the best seat in the house!

Your Musical Director Career Adventure Starts Here

EXPLORE IT!

Use your Internet search skills to find out more about the following:

What a musical director actually does

Common musical symbols that appear on a score

The most popular scores from hit Broadway musicals

TRY IT!

Musical Life Story

What if there were a Broadway show about a typical day in your life? What would the background music sound like? Consider what styles of music might enhance all the drama and action—the soundtrack to your life! Assemble a playlist of songs to match everything from getting up and going to school to the bus ride home and that ongoing spat you have with your sib.

Tickle the Ivories

Most musical directors know how to play piano. If you're lucky enough to have one at home, sit down at the keyboard and pick out the melody to a song you like. If you don't have a piano, you can play a virtual one at www.gamekidgame.com/music_games/piano.

PRODUCER

Producer needed to handle business side of blockbuster Broadway show. Multitasking skills required. Must have experience successfully pitching projects to investors, along with excellent marketing and advertising skills. Will be responsible for budget and contracts. Only a top-notch team builder, with a nose for sniffing out potential hit projects, need apply.

- *Ready to take on this challenge?*
  Turn to page 14.

- *Want to explore a career as a Set Designer instead?*
  Go to page 17.

- *Rather consider other choices?*
  Return to page 4.

Explore how Broadway works at **http://bit.ly/ historyofbroadway**.

Find It!

As the **producer** of a Broadway production, your focus is on the three F's: *finding it, funding it, and filling the seats*. The first step is finding the right project. You enjoy reading through mountains of script submissions, hoping to find one with promise. You also attend workshops, low-budget productions of plays or musicals staged to test an audience's reactions and to attract producers' interest. All the while, looking for your next big hit!

Over the years, you develop a kind of "Spidey sense" for potential hits. Finally, at a tiny downtown theater, you see a show that has it all: a fresh idea, great characters, and a spectacular story that will translate well onto the bigger Broadway stage. You've got goose bumps—this is the one!

Fund It!

Now you need to convince other people to believe—and invest!—in your vision. An important part of your job is raising enough money to produce a show. You have to find investors willing to fund your new project. At the **pitch** meeting you are very persuasive, and investors agree to back the show. Woo-hoo! Show me the money!

Now it's time to roll up your sleeves and get down to the business of producing a Broadway show! You need a director, choreographer, stage manager, composer, musical director, costume and set designer who can all work together to breathe life into the story.

Collaboration is essential to a successful production. Your team will enlist the show's cast members, compose the music, write the lyrics, design the set and costumes, and create a gazillion other elements that make this production unique. Recruiting the right talent for the right jobs can make or break your show.

Fill the Seats

At last, the show is in rehearsals and scheduled to open in a month. Filling the seats is the final piece of your job. Now all your show needs is an audience! There are many advertising and promotional decisions to make. What should the show's publicity poster look like? How much can you spend on newspaper ads? What about a TV spot? Can you book the show's stars on a popular talk show to get some buzz going?

All your hard work pays off. Ticket sales are excellent. At the show's **premiere,** you have butterflies in your stomach, but you know you have done everything possible to make this a hit. It's showtime!

Your Producer Career Adventure Starts Here

EXPLORE IT!

Use your Internet search skills to find out more about the following:

The history of the "Great White Way"

The smash Broadway musical The Producers

Famous Broadway flops

TRY IT!

Choose Your Creative Team

You'll need an awesome team to bring your show to the stage. If you were putting on a play at your school (or even in your backyard), which of your classmates or friends would you assign to the following positions?

Director   *Choreographer*

Set designer   *Songwriter and lyricist*

Costume designer *Stage manager*

Pitch It!

Choose a favorite book, and write a pitch explaining why it would make a great Broadway show.

SET DESIGNER

Creative construction whiz wanted to design and build sets for Broadway play. Experience with 3-D model construction and computer-aided design (CAD) a plus. Work must result in safe, spectacular sets that make audiences feel they are part of the show. Knowledge of history and architecture highly desired. Bring your imagination—and your toolbox!

- *Ready to take on this challenge?*
  Turn to page 18.

- *Want to explore a career as a Stage Actor instead?*
  Go to page 21.

- *Rather consider other choices?*
  Return to page 4.

Meet a Broadway set designer at **http://bit.ly/ Broadwayset**.

An Imaginary World

It's almost time for your meeting with the producer, who hired you to create sets for a new Broadway play. As you read through the script again, images and ideas bloom in your mind.

You are an experienced **set designer** and have worked on historical sets in the past. Those required lots of research to make the sets look authentic. But this play is different. It is a fantasy, so your work requires far more imagination and, well, whimsy. You have ideas, but you have to listen closely as the director describes his vision for the production. Somehow you must mesh what you "see" with what the director expects.

Model Behavior

Luckily you're a pretty good artist, because you have to create a sketch of each scene. From the sketches, you use computer design programs to help everyone visualize how the finished set will look. Using the computer for this makes it easier to make changes once the costume and lighting designers, makeup people, and props masters weigh in with their ideas. It takes teamwork to get all the components right.

Once you have a good sense of how the final set should look, you work with assistants in your design studio to build a scale model of the set. This is a small version made of paper and cardboard, that let's you move the different parts around to see what works best.

From Page to Stage

Once your plans are finalized, skilled workers engineer and build the actual set based on your designs. It takes about five weeks to build the set for a Broadway show. Sometimes you work in your studio, and sometimes you're on set to check that everything is running smoothly.

Running underneath the stage is a system of cables that pull pieces of the scenery on and off the stage. Mishaps with the set can cause miscues, or even injuries, among the cast members. You must make sure everything about the set will go smoothly and safely.

When everything is ready, the entire cast and crew gather for a technical rehearsal. Fortunately, problems are usually minor at this phase so your team has plenty of time to fix them. You look forward to opening night, when you get to see how the audience responds to the world you've created!

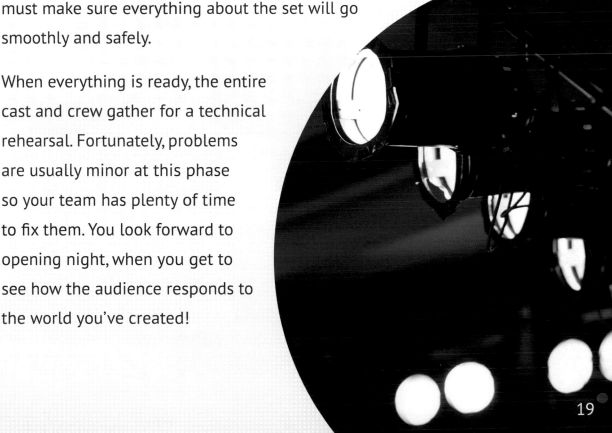

Your Set Designer Career Adventure Starts Here

EXPLORE IT!

Use your Internet search skills to find out more about the following:

The history of theatrical scenery

Tony Award-winning set designers

Different types of stages—proscenium, thrust, arena

TRY IT!

The Look of the Past

David Korins, the set designer for the musical *Annie,* created sets that suggest New York City during the Great Depression of the 1930s. Pick a historical period from the past. Ancient Greece? The California gold rush? Research the appearance of that time and place. Look for images of interior and exterior scenes in old photographs, art books, and online sources. Make a collage of the images you find.

Build It!

Create a scale model of a stage set in a sideways shoebox. You can use doll furniture, Legos™, or build props out of cardboard—stretch your imagination! Cut a long slit along the top, where you can slide in different cardboard backgrounds to change the scenery.

STAGE ACTOR

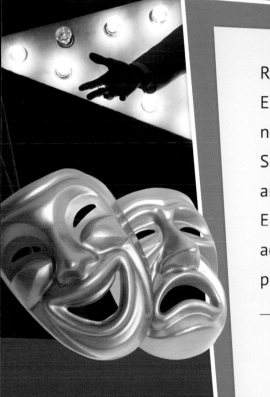

Ready to see your name in lights on Broadway? Experienced stage actor needed for hot, new Broadway-bound musical production. Seeking a triple threat who can sing, dance, and act up a storm. Must belong to Actors' Equity. Professional training a plus. Send acting portfolio to the casting director. Come prepared to impress!

- *Ready to take on this challenge?*
  Turn to page 22.

- *Want to explore a career as a Stage Manager instead?*
  Go to page 25.

- *Rather consider other choices?*
  Return to page 4.

Meet some kid actors in Broadway shows at **http://bit.ly/ Broadwaykids**.

Nailing the Audition

Your agent called. You've been invited to audition for a new Broadway show! You memorize a short scene from the script.

The casting committee includes the show's producer, director, musical director, and choreographer. They are seated on one side of a long table to watch your audition. You are a little nervous but, hey, you are a **stage actor**! You act as if you are totally confident until you relax and get into the role.

You give the audition your all and think you nailed it. The casting committee agree because the next day, you get a **callback**. They want you to star in the show!

Reaching the Back Row

Acting onstage requires more physical skill and energy than acting onscreen. Movements and emotions have to be exaggerated, larger-than-life. Whether you're speaking or singing, you have to project your voice so even audience members in the back row of the theater can hear you clearly. The microphone you wear helps extend your range, saving strain on your voice.

Another big difference between acting on stage and acting in films is that theater actors must perform the same scenes night after night for long-running Broadway productions. Screen actors, on the other hand, are on set for a few weeks or months or until filming is complete and then "it's a wrap."

You attend weeks of rehearsals, starting with a read-through of the script. Then you and the cast work with the director and the choreographer on the **blocking** of different scenes. Markers are placed on the floor so each actor knows where to stand in each scene.

Getting It Right

Rehearsals are going well, and the actors are all "off book," meaning you have all memorized your lines. In a live performance, the audience might notice any mistakes you make, like a missed **cue** or a wrong note. There are no retakes—you just have one chance to get it right in each live performance! So you work hard to learn your part.

As **dress rehearsal** approaches, you are busy with final costume fittings and run-throughs of the show on a finished set. You're so busy that each night you practically fall asleep before your head hits the pillow!

Places, everyone! It's time for your Broadway **debut**!

Your Stage Actor Career Adventure Starts Here

EXPLORE IT!

Use you Internet search skills to find out more about the following:

Famous Broadway stars of the past and present

The Actors' Equity Association

Differences between stage acting and screen acting

TRY IT!

Prepare a Monologue

Choose a short scene from a play or book you like. Practice it again and again in front of a mirror until you have it memorized. Use appropriate movements and gestures to enhance the words. When you're ready, perform the monologue in front of an audience—your family, your best friend, your dog?

Improv, Anyone?

A fun improvisational, or "improv," activity often used in drama school is called "The Expert." Come up with a list of subjects such as cereal, France, scuba diving. Gather some friends and take turns pretending to speak as experts on each subject. Everyone says whatever comes into his or her head, no matter how ridiculous, and keeps talking for a full minute.

STAGE MANAGER

Do you thrive on chaos? Seeking super-organized individual with small ego, big heart, and technical background in theater to work as a stage manager. Must be happy with behind-the-scenes status to keep the show running without a hitch. Are you a skilled people wrangler, who can keep track of a thousand things at once? Please apply!

- *Ready to take on this challenge?*
  Turn to page 26.

- *Want to explore a career as a Director instead?*
  Go to page 5.

- *Rather consider other choices?*
  Return to page 4.

Meet the stage managers of the wildly popular Broadway musical *Wicked* at **http://bit.ly/ Wickedsetdesigner**.

Supporting Roles

Pssst... Want in on a little-known secret about Broadway shows? During a performance there are always more people backstage than onstage. In a large production, more than a hundred people may be hard at work behind the scenes. Somebody needs to make sure every member of the cast and crew does his or her job properly. That person is you, the **stage manager**.

The producer hires you to oversee everything that happens backstage during a theatrical production. You're right at the director's elbow while the show takes shape, and you schedule and run all the rehearsals.

If an actor forgets a piece of dialogue in the middle of a scene, he turns to you and says, "Line." The actress playing the lead role wears twelve different wigs during the show? You need to tell her exactly when her wig fitting is scheduled.

Let's Get Technical

You, as stage manager, rule the roost backstage. You are never without your **prompt book**—a fat binder with a master copy of the script. It's where you keep track of the blocking, as well as all the production's lighting, sound, and set change cues. You'd be lost without your binder—and so would everyone else!

Your desk in the control booth gives you the best view of what happens onstage. From here you give verbal cues through a headset to the lighting and sound technicians. You work closely with the stage crew to devise an efficient plan for every set change—you can't have **stagehands** crashing into one another in the dark between scenes!

You're On!

Once the show opens, you take over for the director. Your job is to make sure every performance goes smoothly for the rest of the play's **run**. Are all the actors present? If someone is late, you might have to call in an **understudy** to substitute for that role.

After today's performance, you put together a written report: *A prop used in Act Two is broken and must be fixed before the next show. One of the chorus members missed a cue—luckily, the audience didn't notice.*

As the actors take their bows, you pat yourself on the back. All that wild applause is for you too, after all!

Your Stage Manager Career Adventure Starts Here

EXPLORE IT!

Use your Internet search skills to find out more about the following:

A checklist of a stage manager's duties

What happens at a technical rehearsal

How to make a "prompt book"

TRY IT!

Block It!

"Blocking notation" is the code stage managers use in their prompt books to track the movements of actors and props onstage. Can you guess what the following blocking notations mean?

1. *Ent UR*   3. *X URC*

2. *X L3*   4. *Kn CS*

(Answers: 1. Enter upstage right, 2. Cross to the left 3 steps, 3. Cross up right center, 4. Kneel center stage)

Be Prepared!

A good stage manager is always prepared. Assemble a stage manager's toolbox, including pens and pencils, chalk, masking tape, a flashlight and extra batteries, first-aid supplies, and emergency sewing supplies (in case an actor has a "wardrobe malfunction").

WRITE YOUR OWN CAREER ADVENTURE

THEATRE
STAGE DOOR

WRITE YOUR OWN CAREER ADVENTURE

You just read about six awesome Broadway careers:

- Director
- Musical director
- Producer
- Set designer
- Stage actor
- Stage manager

Which is your favorite? Pick one, and imagine what it would be like to do that job. Now write your own career adventure!

_____

_____

_____

_____

_____

_____

_____

_____

Go online to download free activity sheets at www.cherrylakepublishing.com/activities.

GLOSSARY

audition tryout for a role in a movie, orchestra, or play

blocking process of arranging moves to be made by the actors during the play

break a leg theatrical slang for good luck

call back invitation to return for a second audition or interview

composer person who writes music

cue signal to say some lines or do something in a play or musical

director person who supervises the actors, camera crew, and other staff for a movie, play, television program, or similar production

dress rehearsal last rehearsal of a play, performed in full costume

debut first public appearance, as in an acting debut

Great White Way nickname for a section of Broadway in Midtown Manhattan

lyricist person who writes the words to a song or musical

monologue long speech delivered by one person

musical director person responsible for the musical aspects of a performance, production, or organization, typically the conductor or leader of a music group

orchestra pit area around or below the stage that houses the musicians

pitch talk meant to persuade someone to do or buy something, as in a sales pitch

premiere first public performance of a show

producer person responsible for the financial and managerial aspects of making of a movie or broadcast or for staging a play or opera

prompt book copy of a play with lots of reminder notes that a stage manager uses during a performance

prop object used on stage or on screen by actors during a performance or screen production

rehearsal practice or trial performance of a play or performance

run sequence of performances of the same production

script the written text of a play

set designer person who designs the physical surroundings in which a theatrical production takes place

stage actor person who tells a story by portraying a character in a theatrical production

stagehands members of the stage crew who are responsible for moving props or scenery during the show

stage manager person who provides practical and organizational support to the director, actors, designers, stage crew and technicians throughout a production

understudy alternate cast member who can substitute for a principal performer in case of illness or other reasons

INDEX

ABOUT THE AUTHOR

Monique Vescia worked in children's book publishing for many years before embarking on her own career as a writer. She is the author of twenty-five non-fiction books on a variety of subjects, ranging from A (animal behavior) to Z (author Markus Zusak) and nearly everything in between. She lives in Seattle, Washington, with her husband and teenage son, and she keeps bees in her own backyard.